CROSSING THE OCEAN OF GRIEF

How to Save Yourself From the Depths of Despair After Losing Someone You Love

Sandy Lotz-Weiner

Title: Crossing the Ocean of Grief: How to Save Yourself From the Depths of Despair After Losing Someone You Love

By: Sandy Lotz-Weiner

ISBN for Print: 979-8-218-29347-5

For permissions, contact:

sandy@sandylotzweiner.com

Cover design: Rhianon Paige

Editing: Dustin Dixon

Published by: AFGO Press

Printed in the United States

First Edition 2023

NOTICE: The information provided in this book is not to be construed as a substitute for medical advice or professional services of any kind. It is for educational purposes only. Neither the author nor the publisher make any representations or warranties, express or implied, about the accuracy, completeness, reliability, suitability, or availability with respect to the information, products, services, or related materials contained in this book for any purpose. The advice and strategies contained herein may not be suitable for your particular situation. Any use of this information is at your own risk.

This book is dedicated to those who have crossed their own ocean of grief.

Thank you for sharing your stories and your wisdom with me.

TABLE OF CONTENTS

A PERSONAL MESSAGE FROM ME TO YOU

Dear Reader,

First, I would like to say how sorry I am for what you are going through right now—my deepest condolences to you and your loved ones. My wish for you is to find peace after the pain, and I hope that you find the support and guidance you are looking for here. It is for you that I wrote this book. I am also very grateful that you have picked up my book, Crossing the Ocean of Grief, and I hope you find solace as I share my personal story of navigating my way through the depths of despair.

I am confident that you are stronger and more resilient than you feel right now. My book will introduce you to my Life Raft Model, which is the foundation of my work. It is meant to keep you afloat during the grief storms you encounter as you cross your own Ocean of Grief. I will be swimming alongside you.

I, too, once felt like I was drowning. In fact, I wasn't sure I wanted to live. I didn't believe it was possible to come back from feeling so helpless and hopeless.

I invite you to take my Life Raft Growth Assessment to help you navigate your way back to life, even when you can't imagine what the future holds.

You will find a copy of the LRG Assessment on my website at www.sandylotzweiner.com.

With love,
Sandy Lotz-Weiner

"And the day came when the risk to remain tight in the bud was more painful than the risk to Blossom."

~ Anais Nin

INTRODUCTION

Grief Has Its Own Agenda

"Just come home."

Three simple words that would change my life forever.

Being summoned home like that, with no other explanation, can only mean something terrible has happened.

The absolute worst thing, in fact.

In a heartbeat, life as I knew it was over.

Literally.

My husband's heart had stopped beating, and in 8-tenths of a second, my whole world became silent and still.

On April 29th, 2017, on a beautiful spring morning, my beloved Tony, husband, and partner of almost 30 years, passed away suddenly and unexpectedly.

In the coming hours, days, weeks, and months, I wasn't sure if I could live without him.

I didn't know if I wanted to live at all.

The morning after Tony's funeral, I couldn't get out of bed. I had tightly curled myself up in a ball, wishing every breath I took would be my last.

That's when I heard my mother's voice in my head.

"Get up, my child, brush your hair, put on some lipstick; you have guests coming."

So I did.

Thank you, Mom.

⁂

I did what I had to do to get through the days and weeks that followed, leaning on the support available and letting the reality of my so-called "new normal" set in. Dazed and confused, I walked around my condo feeling completely lost, unmoored, and adrift.

I begged and pleaded with my employer for time off to heal before I had to return to work. Three days of paid bereavement was hardly enough after losing a spouse who was *my world*.

My rock.

My heart.

I borrowed time by cashing in my vacation days, even risking losing my job. I knew I needed to take care of myself before I could phase into the world again if I could even find a way to take that first phase back into "my life."

My life without Tony.

The reality of him being gone forever would hit me like a tsunami of emotions.

I tried to surf those waves but found myself getting pulled down again.

And again.

And again. The waves cut through me like shards of glass.

"Maybe these broken shards will become beautiful sea glass," I told my counselor one day.

But who was I kidding? The waves just kept on coming.

Life after loss comes with enormous challenges, and there were many of them. Dealing with grief while reentering and participating in life again was excruciating at times.

On days when I thought maybe, just maybe, I might find my sea legs again, boom!

I was sucked underwater again.

And again.

And again.

If you picked up this book hoping I would paint you an inspiring picture of grief, like so many books out there tend to do, I'm afraid I can't do that.

I'm here to tell you the absolute truth about grief.

I will walk with you every step of the way.

I suspect that if you're reading this, you've already found out that grief can be messy and confusing, hitting you from out of nowhere with a velocity that can knock the wind out of you.

You can be coasting along when another "first" hits you. The first wedding anniversary without my husband. The first birthday - his, and then mine. He would have no more candles to blow out, and I never cared if I ever had another birthday cake again. The truth is, I didn't care about anything.

If you are reading this, I'm sure you understand. Your life may feel very dark and uncertain right now.

Please know this: I am so sorry for your loss and that you have to go through this. It may be too soon for me to tell you that you will be okay, so I will refrain for now. However, if you stick with me until the end of this tiny book, you may find another word for how you feel, one that is even the tiniest bit more hopeful.

Consider this book a tiny life raft where you don't have to pretend everything is okay. That is entirely up to you.

My hope is that you will decide that, at the very least, there will be another life for you after loss, grief, and despair.

I speak from experience, as you can tell. I know this because I have had to find my way through it alone. Since then, I have helped many others navigate those waters.

That is the new inspired life that I found after loss, and I would love nothing more than to help you find your way there, too.

❧

Having lost my Dad at 23 and learning that I could not outrun or numb my pain, I knew I wanted to do grief differently this time. I did not want to white-knuckle through it or pretend I was fine.

I wanted to slow down and face it.

I wanted to "get better, not bitter."

I didn't know what this meant, what it could look like, or how to get there.

But I did know that it was what I needed, and I was determined to find a way.

I was prepared to let grief hollow me out and fill me up with compassion.

"I'll paddle into the storm, not away from it this time."

I would learn how to console myself, soothe my soul, and heal my broken heart.

But grief had its own agenda.

"Not so fast," it said.

And so began my journey into the depths of grief and a whole new way of being me. Grief became my teacher.

I do not intend for this book to sound like so many others:

"You can do it."

"Give it time."

"Embrace the suffering."

"There's a light at the end of the tunnel."

Frankly, all that talk did nothing to help me. *Nothing.*

People's intentions were good, of course, and the books I read offered soothing words, but grief would not be rushed, coerced, or manipulated.

Grief refused to be fooled.

If I managed to distract myself, grief was always there waiting for me.

After reading many books and listening to so many "experts" on the topic of healing after the loss of someone you loved, I decided to establish a different relationship with grief. As a Certified Life Coach who has been through deep grief more than once, I knew this challenge would need my full attention. It would not serve me to run away from this unbearable pain.

I needed to understand it.

Then, I needed to accept it because it wasn't going away.

Next, I had to take responsibility for what would happen: I'd either succumb to the pain of grief or become wiser, kinder, and more compassionate because of it.

Finally, and only after I was able to move through this process *deliberately*, could I decide where I wanted to go and what I wanted to do.

We all tend to want to skip the first three phases.

We want to run from the pain of it all.

And taking responsibility? Who has the energy for that?

So I took it slowly. Some days, I put my lipstick on, but mostly, I allowed the pain to be there.

Eventually, I began to recognize a pattern in the way I was dealing with my grief, and through much trial and error, I began to structure it in a way that would eventually become a model that I live by.

I call it my **Life Raft Model,** and it's what allowed me to navigate the turbulent waters of crippling grief so that I could once again stand firmly on dry land.

The Life Raft Model consists of four distinct phases:

Phase 1: Drowning in Sorrow | *"I can't survive this."*

In the early stages of grief, we're not sure we can survive. In fact, we don't know if we even *want* to survive. This is where we begin.

Phase 2: Learning to Stay Afloat | *"Maybe I can survive this."*

Learning to live without our loved ones is a very painful experience. It is necessary for us to take the time we need to adjust to our "new reality." Accepting what has happened can be extremely difficult, so moving into Phase 2 is a process, more than a place, and it's where we commit to healing our broken hearts. It is the only chance we have to find peace.

Phase 3: Paddling as Fast as I Can | *"I am going to survive. Now what?"*

Responsibility: Yes, we will all need support during grief, but we must find the right support for ourselves and commit to doing our grief work. We can't control or predict our grief.

We can heal, but we must be prepared to take the responsibility of healing upon ourselves.

Phase 4: Back on Dry Land | *"I am alive!"*

Our purpose in life did not die with our beloved; we still have a future. Phase 4 is our chance to reinvest in our new reality fully. We need a new vision for ourselves in this life. It begins with hope and grows when we make the *right* choices and take the *right* actions.

My Life Raft Model saved me, but only because there was a part of me that knew I did not want to die despite those dark days of deep despair.

I wanted to feel free from my pain and move away from the dark towards the light. I wanted something different than where I was at the time. I wanted things to change, so I knew *I* needed to change.

I needed to see a future that inspired me, where there was a field of new possibilities. A place where I could feel fully alive and experience peace, love, and joy again. I wanted to HEAL.

I know how badly you want that, too.

The Life Raft Model differs from so many grief "instructions" out there because it takes you on a journey that not only heals but also transports you to a new place of expansion and growth.

This framework not only focuses on surviving your loss and restoring you to your previous level of existence but also on growing through grief. You see, I don't believe we are meant to go through all this heartache and pain to stay the same person.

How can we?

Even though I feel that "parts" of me died with my husband that day, I kept breathing.

Somehow, I kept living.

I am still here. Today, I am a different woman. I feel stronger than before and have had to do things I thought were impossible.

I see life through different eyes today. I am acutely aware of the fragility of life and that this life is made up of precious moments. And, we all get ONLY this one beautiful life to live to the fullest.

When we stay curious, courageous, and open to possibilities, we can find ways to resolve the pain of our loss. This allows us to feel free, joyful, and at peace, ready to write our next chapter and claim our lives back.

So, I invite you to come on this healing journey with me. No matter where you are in your personal Grief journey, we start right where you are. I will share all that I have learned, what worked, and all the things I tried that I hoped would create a shortcut to my ultimate survival.

Hop in this life raft with me. I know it's scary. I know you want the pain to stop.

Let's take it one phase at a time.

May you choose hope to heal.

"She could never go back and make some of the details pretty. All she could do was move forward and make the whole beautiful."

~Terri St Cloud

THE LIFE RAFT MODEL

I once had a dream where Tony and I found ourselves in the middle of the ocean in open waters. We'd fallen out of a boat, and no land was in sight. We were gripped with fear.

In real life, we had left our homeland to build a life in the United States. We felt lost at sea. We asked ourselves, *"What have we done?"*

The dream represented my anxiety. We had to find a way to survive, so we made a makeshift life raft from the debris floating around us and somehow managed to get on top and start to paddle. We had no other choice.

Similarly, my life without Tony, one of pain, fear, isolation, and uncertainty, would not change until I built my own life raft. I could not continue going through my days as if I were lost at sea, alone in deep open water again.

Then I remembered that dream of 14 years ago. And that's when

I realized I needed to build a life raft for myself, something that could keep me safe and afloat until I could get to a "safe harbor" again.

Grief is neither linear nor logical. On the contrary, it's rather messy and chaotic. My Life Raft Model gave me a sense of something tangible and solid that I could hold close and revisit day after day so that I could keep myself afloat long enough to get out of the deep waters of despair.

I had to cycle through the 4 phases more than once. As my awareness increased, so did my need for acceptance, and with that came new personal responsibilities. Everything kept changing, but I knew I was growing, albeit slowly, and with that, my world started to expand as well until, one day, I found myself back on dry land.

Here's a glimpse at the 4 phases of the model that saved my life and gave me a new sense of purpose.

Phase 1: DROWNING IN SORROW | *"I Can't Survive This"*

"What is happening to me? I feel awful, I can't sleep, I can't eat, I can't breathe! Am I losing my mind?"

Grief will show up with many symptoms, not just emotionally but also mentally and physically. Our bodies will take a hit for sure. Grief can last longer than we want it to. It's essential to slow down and take stock of our situation in the most rational way possible.

We need to find the proper support for this journey and learn as much as we can about this new, unfamiliar landscape we must navigate.

"What do I need in this moment to get myself to the next one? What do I need to make it through the day? To keep going?"

Phase 2: LEARNING TO STAY AFLOAT | *"Maybe I Can Survive This"*

This loss is permanent.

Tony is not coming back. That part of my life is over.

But I am still here. Why? I want to have one more day, but I can't.

Did I say everything I wanted to? Did I do everything I meant to?

Did I love enough?

Was I loved? Yes, of course I was.

Why was I not home that day?

What could I have done differently, better, more?

I walked myself through these questions in my mind a million times a day. I did not find the answers I desperately wanted. The storm inside of me kept growing, subsiding momentarily, only to flare up again with gale-force intensity.

I let it rage.

Eventually, I surrendered to the reality of "what is." I allowed myself to break open. I stopped resisting my reality. No longer holding back the complex emotions, I sat with my pain. Somewhere in those difficult moments, I realized my life would go on.

My relationship with Tony would continue, albeit on a different plane.

Love never dies. Our loved ones will never be forgotten; they live forever in our hearts and memories. They guide us from afar.

As I allowed myself to slowly accept all of this, I began to feel a sense of peace again.

Phase 3: PADDLING AS FAST AS I CAN | *"I Will Survive This."*

Surviving, like healing, is a choice we make.

It is up to us to ensure our survival, just as it is up to us to heal. Not only is it within our power to do so, but it is the only way to *truly* do so.

We must find healthy coping skills to comfort and soothe our souls. We have to commit to moving ourselves forward, paddling and paddling, one stroke at a time.

Some days, we will stall and go nowhere, and that's okay. Heck, it might feel like we are going in circles sometimes or even staying in place.

We begin again. Remember, we are committed to getting ourselves out of the deep waters and into the calmer seas that lead back to dry land.

This is where we are heading. This is the plan. In Phase 3, we are committed to doing anything to make this happen.

Because we finally believe we can.

Phase 4: BACK ON DRY LAND | *"I Am Alive"*

After what will feel like a long journey of deep inner work and endless paddling, suddenly, we will look up and see land in sight.

Let's explore this new place and find some company.

At last, we will no longer be alone. That will feel so good. We are exhausted, yet we feel so proud of ourselves, immensely grateful for how far we have come, and motivated to build a new chapter. We are starting to see the endless new possibilities for ourselves.

Our loved ones will always be with us, but by this phase in the model, we realize we still have a life to live.

Working through our grief and letting go of our pain is a process. We have to do each phase by itself and one at a time before we can start to think about building a new chapter. We might be tempted to jump ahead of ourselves to the next phase. This can sound very alluring. I know I was tempted.

A word of warning: Please don't rush through just to get to the "other side." It will likely only end up taking even longer to get there.

Take time to catch your breath, find your footing, and recenter yourself as you move through each phase.

Think of mountain climbers; their journey to the summit begins in base camp. The same is true for us. Without laying the right foundation for our healing and growth, we risk losing everything and having to start over, or we just get stuck.

We need to take the time to set this up correctly. Each phase will unfold into the next, at the right time and in the right order. With each step comes new insight, wisdom, and responsibility.

Once we master this, we're ready to move on.

That is how we get clarity; it is how we allow the Life Raft Model to guide us. Our job is to trust the healing process and believe in ourselves so we might dance again one day.

Besides, we'll never be able to dance if we don't first learn how to stand on our own two feet again, right?

❦

For me, it began because I could not get my dream about our raft out of my head. The similarities were so apparent.

Just like then, I felt overwhelmed by my emotions – underwater, drowning in emotion; I needed that life raft again! Only this time, I would be paddling alone. It was up to me to get myself through this storm back to safety on dry land.

And that is why I call this my Life Raft Model.

I believe it offers a whole new way to look at grief and its profound impact on us.

When I first sought relief from the depths of despair, I found teachings that made me feel even more despondent. They suggested that I would "get used to my pain" and "learn to live with it" or even "grow bigger than my pain."

I did not want to hear this. It sounded hopeless, and it made me feel helpless. I believed that if I could understand and resolve my pain, I could create an entirely new and meaningful chapter in my life.

I have always approached life this way. After I lost my Dad, I lived to experience almost 30 beautiful years with Tony, a life better than I could have imagined.

So when Tony died, there was a glimmer of hope that I might go on to create another meaningful chapter with the next phase of my life, although it took me a while to get there.

But I was not just going to merely *survive* the loss; I wanted to thrive again.

Many grief programs focus on acceptance. Of course, acceptance is a vital phase and one that is an important part of the Life Raft Model, but it is only part of the grief journey.

What about joy?

There is more, and it can be beautiful.

I take my clients through a growth journey as we tackle the heavy topic of grief. I believe the better informed my clients are, the better the decisions they will make.

Understanding why I felt the way I did when I lost Tony reduced my resistance to grief and allowed me to trust the process and let go. My fear became less paralyzing, and healing became possible. I teach not only how to heal from such a devastating loss but also how to grow and eventually thrive.

We can evolve.

It is possible to fill the void left by the loss.

We can remember our loved ones with more love than pain. It is possible to move from grief to gratitude for the love you experienced.

Over time, you will be able to once again live a life with meaning and purpose, one where you can create new experiences, be joyful, and live in peace.

It's understandable to feel reluctant to commit to crossing the Ocean of Grief. After all, it's agonizingly painful. It's the hardest work we will ever do in life.

We think it won't work; maybe we know someone who tried and gave up, so we think it is impossible.

Finding the right support is crucial. Looking for a role model can be a great inspiration. I ultimately realized I am still here and my life matters. Nothing would change until I decided to do the work, for as long as it takes, until I got to the other side.

Very early on in my grief journey, when the pain was intense, I told my therapist friend, "I am prepared to try anything to feel better," and she said, *"Your willingness to do what it takes is the key."*

When we are willing to do the work, no matter what, we will succeed.

Another major consideration for me was gratitude. I had to dig deep for this, and once I could find some gratitude for my life, my energy started to shift, and I began to look at life more optimistically.

There is a lot of support out there, but be sure you get the *right* support. After all, grief needs to be properly witnessed. While people mean well, not everyone is grief-aware.

We might need more support than they can give us. I worked with a grief expert very early on because I recognized that I needed to get back on my feet quickly. I had to go back to work and wanted to ensure I was okay enough to do so. By some miracle, my coach happened to be a widow herself, which was of tremendous value to me. She understood me, had been in my shoes, and was still here.

She was proof that I could survive.

The road is long and trying, and without the right kind of support, I would likely have given up. Once I started to feel better and knew I was going to make it, I also knew I wanted to support others like me. No one should go through this alone.

If at any time while you're reading this book you'd like to reach out for some support, I've provided some options for you in the

"Where Do We Go From Here?" chapter; feel free to skip ahead and reach out to me.

So, are you ready to take this journey with me? I will paddle alongside you. I was once where you are today. I was lucky and found myself an experienced guide.

Now, I am here to support you on your journey. Let's cross this ocean together.

"It's always darkest before the dawn."

~Thomas Fuller

PHASE 1: LOST AT SEA

"I Don't Think I Can Survive This."

It's true. I really didn't think I could survive.

If I'm being honest, I didn't know if I even wanted to survive.

The loss was too much to bear. I couldn't even comprehend it.

Coming to terms with such a loss seems impossible. For me, this meant starting where I was by acknowledging the enormity of my loss and becoming aware of how my body was responding to my grief.

I noticed how I was holding my breath when the waves of emotions washed over me – how my mind started to panic, wanting to run ahead of itself, spinning out of control. Unless I could steady my breath and let those emotions move through me, I would surely drown.

I knew I had to hold on to my center somehow. Over time, I learned that my breath and my body would become my most significant allies. I had to remember this and care for my body as best I could.

I had to practice *mindful awareness.*

Where my heart used to be became a big aching hole. I kept trying to protect it, to keep it from breaking more, but I could not.

With every big loss, there will be many secondary losses yet to be revealed to us as time goes by. Each loss cuts us a bit deeper. Without the ability to practice mindful awareness, I found myself lost at sea, without a life raft in sight. I suffered terribly because I didn't realize it was safe to feel these emotions as long as I continued breathing.

There were many times I wanted to run away from the emotions or numb them to keep them at bay. I never won these battles; grief would always catch up with me and demand attention.

However, when I remembered to breathe and trust my body, I felt a little less lost. When I forgot to breathe, I would lose touch with the very moment I was in, and my mind would panic as the emotions swept over me once more.

It is all too easy to spiral down from here into the lonely darkness where no light could enter. A place where I was scared of running out of energy and air, of being dragged under by the heaviness of it all and slowly sinking to the bottom.

Have you ever felt this way, dear reader? Have you ever found yourself caught completely unaware by the sheer depth of your loss?

On the other side of loss and grief awaits another chapter and a new you. However, unless we resolve our pain, we risk dragging it into our future or staying lost between two worlds, never fully living again.

Before we can even begin to imagine that new chapter of our world, we must come to grips with where we are *right now,* what has happened, and how it is affecting us.

If we are ever going to begin resolving that pain and growing through grief, it must begin with mindful awareness. Reminding ourselves of not only what is gone but also what still remains. If we don't take stock, we cannot ever heal. For with every fresh wound, our old, unresolved open wounds tend to resurface and demand our attention again.

This is a place where we pause to heal deeper. We don't want to keep dragging old pain into the next chapter. The loss is real; it leaves a deep void. The void we feel is there because what was there before mattered to us and was integral to our lives somehow.

We were blessed by having had this person who shared their lives with us. Rest assured that it is possible to let go of the pain without fearing losing the memories. That will never happen. We will never forget our loved ones; in fact, the more we heal, the more we will remember with less pain and more love.

I know firsthand how difficult it can be when you're lost in the fog of loss. I know that it seems like there could be no way out. But I promise you, there is.

Sometimes, all we need is a guiding light to bring us back to shore. We can only go one breath at a time, one paddle stroke at a time. It's hard, I know. You might feel like giving up.

Please don't.

On my darkest nights, I would remember the saying, "It's always darkest before the dawn." Just before the first light of day breaks, it seems to be awfully dark, then slowly, the light returns, and a new day dawns before our very eyes.

Making our way through this first phase is crucial because it will set us on our path to healing. Mindful awareness allows us to see the truth, the impact of our loss on our lives, and how we respond to it. We will become aware of what we need to support us, what *good support* looks like, and where to find it. Like most new skills, we need to practice to become familiar with it, but this will take some time and patience.

I was tempted to move too fast. I felt that grief was slowing me down; I thought I was losing time somehow. I smile at this today because grief was doing her job, slowing me down to learn the skills I needed not just to survive but to heal, grow, and evolve. Before I could run and walk, I needed to learn to crawl....

One of the ways that this lack of mindful awareness manifests itself is when we absentmindedly go about our same old patterns like our grief isn't there. Ignoring the feeling will not make it go away.

I was like a racehorse waiting for the stable doors to open and run wild, so happy to feel a taste of freedom, to break away. At the first glimpse of feeling even slightly better, I would take on too much or push too hard, only to crash in a couple of days, feeling like I was back where I started. Instead of making progress, I was losing ground again.

The first ray of sunshine does not mean it is summer.

It was a lesson I had to learn more than once. My grief needed tending just like a garden needs water. You see, our capacity is stretched to the limit when adjusting to loss and major life transitions. With each incremental gain, we need time to stabilize and find our footing and confidence before advancing. As I started to gain strength, I wanted to increase my social life and feel part of the world around me. The problem was that I took on too much and too soon. You may experience this, too.

Once we enter back into the world, we will have new experiences with new demands that will overtax us. If we keep moving outwards, we will reach capacity and crash. We need to take time between the high and the low tides to adjust.

The advice is to not make any big changes in your first year after a big loss, and for good reason. We will feel different in the months to come. Early on, my brother invited me to come and stay with him for a while, and I loved hearing that; it felt so good. I also knew that unless I resolved my pain, I would just take it with me somewhere else. I needed to heal first, then make some decisions.

Clarity comes with time.

If we don't take the time to practice mindful awareness, it can lead to less than solid foundations that will not hold us up over time. It might set us up for false starts and many restarts. Mindful awareness is the solid foundation we need to build on as we go forward with our lives.

This is the crucial phase, the big adjustment when learning to focus on our needs despite what is happening around us and what wants to pull us away from our life's work.

Without self-awareness, we have no starting point, only darkness. Once we become aware of the reality of our situation and its problems, there is hope because we will finally understand where our battle begins. As we grow our awareness, we grow with it and see new possibilities.

Knowing the difference between when "to do and when to just be with what is" is important to developing mindful awareness. These valuable lessons will pave the way for us as we move through Grief and toward our healing.

One of the most important things to remember when we practice saving ourselves from drowning is taking our time to observe the fullness of our experience. It is possible to feel conflicting emotions like sadness and gratitude simultaneously.

Phase 1 is understandably painful when we feel "lost at sea." But with mindful awareness, we can find our way back.

We can finally move away from the most turbulent seas and start to think, *"Maybe I can survive this."*

There is a crack in everything/that's how the light gets in."

~Leonard Cohen

PHASE 2: LEARNING TO STAY AFLOAT

"Maybe I Can Survive This."

After suffering two big losses back to back, first Tony and then my Mom, I struggled immensely. Once I came to terms with those losses in my mindful awareness phase, I then learned to practice what I call *graceful acceptance.*

This is the most difficult part of the journey as we cross the Ocean of Grief.

The reason that this phase is so difficult is that we actively fight against it for a while. We don't want to accept what happened.

But, sooner or later, we realize that we don't have a choice. We must sit with the truth of what happened and what is gone forever.

Yes, the truth can take a very long time to sink in.

My first response was to resist what IS and to yearn for what WAS. Maybe that is true for you, too. Sadly, it does not help us one bit.

Kicking and screaming at the reality of my situation was just causing me more pain and suffering. It was only postponing the inevitable.

I had to get to *graceful acceptance*.

But first, I had to come to the full realization that *he was never coming back*.

As hard as we may wish for it, there is no going back to our old lives. We can only go forward... or remain lost at sea.

The sooner we learn to accept where we are and what has happened to us, the greater the chance we will find our grace in the enormity of our loss.

For me, grace is a dance of movement and fluidity. It takes time to find acceptance. At times, we move toward acceptance only to pull further away. We repeat this pattern until we get to full and *graceful* acceptance. The less we resist, the more graceful it becomes.

Yes, at first, we might want to "kick and scream," but it is not until we fully surrender that we can begin to let go of the pain. In order for my Life Raft Model to work, I had to sit with all of my difficult emotions for as long as it took to let them go.

Without a fight.

And then repeat the process all over again. I've coached clients who have cycled through phases one and two over and over again until it finally stuck. This is the way it *needs* to be for the healing to stick.

The experience of grief is not linear. That is what makes it so painful. It's like waves that throw us onto the beach and just as quickly pull us back into the water.

⁊

Living without Tony was unthinkable; the thought was unbearable to me. He was my world. Besides Ms. Cleo, our cat, he was the only family I had in the United States. My early days of grief were filled with nothingness; I felt numb, dazed, and confused most of the time. Waking up every morning to my new reality, I felt sick to my stomach. *"Oh no, it was not a bad dream; this is real."*

It took a very long time for me to accept my loss. It actually began with the polar *opposite* of graceful acceptance.

It began with total resistance to what is.

Mainly because I did not want to or could not bear the painful thought of living a life without Tony.

I resisted facing my pain and accepting the reality of my loss. It was a scary place for me to be, and when I get scared, I tend to freeze. I was somewhere in the middle of the ocean on a life raft all alone.

By some miracle, I became aware that staying here would get me absolutely nowhere. I was so tempted, but I knew I needed to move through this phase as gracefully as possible. Going back was not an option; going forward was the only way.

Just. Keep. Paddling.

Somehow, I began to hope that there might be something new on the horizon for me, just as there is something new out there for you.

Graceful acceptance is the cornerstone of the Life Raft Model because it will set the tone for recovery and healing that is to come. More importantly, it will prevent you from becoming a shipwreck on a deserted beach somewhere, never to be found again.

But why is this phase so difficult, you might ask?

It's because we are being asked to accept our worst nightmare and open ourselves up to feeling unbearable pain.

Something has happened to someone we loved. They have died, and they are gone forever from this world.

Our lives will never be the same again.

It is completely out of our control.

Reading this right now, you may be feeling out of control. Just like our sudden loss, healing is one of those things in life that you can't possibly imagine until it happens.

Say you trained very hard to run a marathon, and one week before the event, you became injured and couldn't compete anymore. Gone is your chance at earning a medal or making a dream come true. You are bitterly disappointed and are forced to sit this one out.

The question becomes: are you going to do so graciously? Or resentfully?

Bitter or better?

How do you want to *be* in your life?

Even though you are not happy about the situation, in order to support your healing and recovery, you inevitably have to come to terms with the situation and *decide*. If you want to be ready for the next opportunity to compete in a marathon, you must give yourself time to heal. This is graceful acceptance. We stop fighting. We bow our heads and accept.

The sad reality of life is that not all our dreams will come true, and sometimes, not even the simplest of plans will work out the way we want them to. Tragedies happen every day. I have worked with clients who have experienced multiple significant losses back to back, with very little time in between to recover.

I know of parents who have lost children in car accidents, overdoses, and suicide. They have managed, some of them with my help, to find the grace to go on. It requires a lot of work, support, and time, that is true.

I have always believed that it is not what happens to us but how we handle what happens to us that matters. I never knew how hard it would be for me to stand by that belief until I was truly tested.

If we try to jump straight into Graceful Acceptance without first undertaking Mindful Awareness, then our acceptance phase will be neither graceful nor complete.

In fact, we may unintentionally be hindering our own progress. We can't accept and acknowledge what we are not aware of yet. Mindful awareness is something that unfolds over time and is naturally followed by graceful acceptance.

As we become aware, we can accept incrementally. We have to crawl before we can walk, right? Moving too quickly throws us off balance; just like a toddler, getting upright and walking will take many attempts and falls.

We can not bypass the pain to get to the next phase, as we have to feel the full intensity of our pain in order to resolve it. Then and only then can we start to integrate the loss into our lives.

Graceful acceptance is a building block that leads to phase 3 because it lays the perfect foundation where we will be called to take personal responsibility and exercise self-agency.

The first 2 phases were about becoming aware and accepting the external circumstances or events that lead to us experiencing all the hard emotions.

Phase 3, however, is about our response to what happened and our internal processes that prepare us to take action. We can't take responsibility for what we are unaware of, and only after we have accepted the full reality of our loss and what we must do to go forward with our lives.

So, as you can see, graceful acceptance is a critical phase in the Life Raft Model. It is the phase that will steer us in the right direction when we do it in the correct order.

We cannot reach our "safe harbor" without allowing ourselves to move through Phases 1 and 2, however long it may take.

How long will this take? It is hard to say. It will be different for all of us. The grief journey will be uniquely our own. Our loss will determine the extent of our grief, and no two losses will ever be the same.

Please know that you can reach out for help at any time. You don't have to do this journey entirely alone. Reach out to me when it feels like you have nowhere else to turn. (My contact information is included at the end of this book.)

Always remember that the goal is to return to dry land, which may take a while. False promises and false hope will invariably backfire.

In Phase 3, when you're ready for it, you'll be in a more powerful position to make choices that serve your best interests as you move. Once you're strong enough, you'll be in a position to take personal responsibility for where you go from here.

"You care so much you feel as though you will bleed to death with the pain of it."

~ J.K. Rowling

PHASE 3: PADDLING AS FAST AS I CAN

"I Will Survive This. Now, What?"

When my phone stopped ringing and my friends and neighbors stopped coming by, I realized I needed to take responsibility for my grief recovery.

They had their own lives to take care of.

And I had mine.

I'd better start paddling.

My two siblings lived 10,000 miles away. It would be too easy to pretend I was doing okay when speaking on the phone. No one was going to come and check in on me.

I knew I had to take care of myself. If I did not take charge of my recovery, no one would.

Easier said than done. This is the phase I call **committed willingness** because it forces us to recognize that it is up to us to heal and discover that next new phase in life that allows us to feel inspired again. But, we must first commit to it completely.

What should I do now? I found myself WAITING for something. A clue, a sign, permission – but for what?

To feel better. I had a feeling that was still going to take a while.

A question I had to ask myself was this: *"Am I willing to feel better?"*

Somehow, committing myself to feeling better seemed harder than staying in pain.

Meanwhile, I had bills to pay. Life went on.

What do I need right NOW? It was an empowering question, I realized.

And so my new life began to unfold. I was finally willing to commit to creating the next chapter of my life.

Because there was really no other choice beyond continuing to live with the ghosts of the past. Was it a crystal clear moment for me? Briefly, yes, but then the fog would come back.

As time passed, I continued to find areas where I could practice my committed willingness, such as showing up in my career, being fully present and on board, and leading my team.

Besides, not only did I need to earn an income, but my life still mattered. Even though I had to return to work sooner than I wanted or was ready for, I learned to feel grateful for this. I fully committed to showing up to serve others and to do whatever it took to care for myself.

Grief can wreak havoc on our health – it affects our emotional, physical, and spiritual well-being. Still, I was determined to stay healthy. I could only go as far as my health would let me, and I knew I wanted to go a long way.

So, this is where I started, with the realization that as long as I kept paddling, I would survive. It was up to me to set my course.

For you, dear reader, recognizing your responsibility in creating that new life might begin somewhere else.

Maybe it will look like cooking for yourself once again.

Maybe it will mean bathing as you once did.

Whatever the small step is, it will eventually lead to bigger and more independent steps as you go.

If you ever want to learn a new language or take up a new hobby, this phase might be the time that you can start to consider it.

"Can I really do that?" you might ask.

Yes, you can.

❧

Committed willingness is perhaps the most crucial phase in writing that new chapter in your inspiring life because it's where we take ownership of our recovery and healing. This is the phase in the Life Raft Model where we get to take charge of our situation more actively for the first time in a long while.

In this phase, we ask ourselves, *"What do I need?"* over and over again until we actually *feel* taken care of.

For me, I needed to find people who could support me in staying accountable – this was the magic key. I found a coach who met me exactly where I was and who was experienced in grief coaching.

Perhaps you've heard the saying, "If you want to go fast, go alone, and if you want to go far, go together"? Well, I knew I wanted to leave my suffering behind. Trying to go fast wasn't going to work. But together with my coach, I could go far in my newfound life raft.

She helped me find responsibility until I was able to do it myself.

Without committed willingness, we tend to stay stuck in the debris of our broken lives. It's like sitting in a pile of ashes.

Rebuilding requires us to *purposefully* clear a new path.

The bottom line for me was that I wanted something different for myself. Staying in my shattered life would surely make me spiral even lower. Even in my suffering, I knew that much. So, I decided that would not be an option for me.

Besides, it was getting increasingly lonely out there alone on my raft. I was committed to making it to dry land.

That's when I started paddling as fast as I could. No one was going to "save" me. This is what makes Phase 3 so difficult: even with a guiding light, it is still up to us to save ourselves.

Eventually, our support system moves on, and there you are, still alone. Some days, it will feel like we've been knocked off our raft into turbulent waters.

Remember what I said about grief? It doesn't move in a straight line; it twists and turns and throws us about. There are days when we second-guess everything and everyone – even those who are still there to lend a helping hand.

There was a time when we trusted that we knew where we were going.

We had plans, and then, BOOM! The tsunami hit.

We have become acutely aware that we don't have control over very much in our lives.

That illusion is gone.

We need to be patient and allow ourselves the time to experience Phases 1 and 2 in order to recenter ourselves long enough to determine what we want and need in this new chapter in our lives.

When I was in Phase 3, paddling as fast as I could, I finally realized that the only person who could actually heal me was *me*. Responsibility forces us to understand that the next chapter of our lives is attainable, but only as long as we are willing to make it happen. When we understand this, we are ready (finally) to write the next chapter.

Not everyone is guaranteed to make it through to Phase 4 unless they promise never to stop paddling, no matter how many times they're thrown overboard or lose their way.

The next and final phase in the Life Raft Model is about taking *inspired action* to live an *inspired life* in a way you never could have imagined, both before your loss or while you're stuck in the depths of despair.

It dawned on me that my *heart* was broken, not my mind or purpose in life. I am still here, so there must be a reason, a plan, a chapter, a life that is still worth living.

I recall hearing the sound of my heart beating. *"Wait, what is that? Could it be that my heart is beating a little stronger?"*

Something that I once thought was impossible to bear eventually became bearable.

Oh my! Could that be land ahead?

"You can't stop the waves, but you can learn to surf."

~Jon Kabat-Zinn

PHASE 4: BACK ON DRY LAND

"I Am Alive!"

One afternoon, while sitting on my couch, still alone, feeling a little sorry for myself and wondering what to do, I heard this voice: *"Your new life will not arrive at your doorstep in an Amazon box."*

This time, I smiled. Again, it was the message to "get up and move into the light" and live an ***inspired life.***

Even early in my grief, I had a desire to create another meaningful chapter with my next phase of life. I did not want to survive only; I wanted to thrive again. I also knew it was not going to be easy. After all, it is a life I had not visualized for myself, yet it was the one precious life I had.

"Okay, fine! If I have to create a new chapter for myself, all by myself, one with meaning and purpose, what would that look like?" Followed immediately by, *"And how on earth will I do that?"*

I don't believe we endure difficult times of loss and grief just to survive. I have always believed we can choose our responses in life, and here, once again, I was asked by the Universe to "walk my talk" under challenging circumstances. Post-traumatic growth is possible after experiencing a shocking life event.

I am living proof.

Only when you take the time and pay attention to your grief can you move through the pain of your loss and experience the next new chapter in your inspired life.

Grief does not go away when ignored or suppressed. Grief will stay in the body, which can significantly impact our health. As a pharmacist and Certified Health Coach, I was very aware of the risks associated with not processing my grief, and I was determined not to lose my health.

Sometimes, we need to be reminded of what's at stake. Phase 4 is about taking a proactive stance against the more sinister side of grief when it's left to wreak havoc on our minds and our bodies.

Phase 4 is when we are inspired to come alive again.

You are still here – drastically changed, perhaps – but here you are.

Who is this new you?

Who have you become?

What will you create as you rise again?

In Phase 4, which I also call *Inspired Living,* we are finally starting to see how far we have come and how close we are to living fully again. When we follow Phases 1 through 3 *in the right order,* and we spend the required time in each phase (only your grief knows how long that will be), we will have the perfect foundation for our new chapter.

Once we have made our way to Phase 4, we are ready to take the kind of action that will lead us to create something new for ourselves. Until now, we have been focused on caring for our mental and emotional health. The focus has been on what's going on on *the inside.*

Once we're back on dry land, we can start thinking about what we want to do.

Taking action that leads to an inspired new life doesn't seem as scary or impossible as it may have seemed immediately after our loss.

That is why it is crucial to do the inner work before we try to take any action we are not ready for.

The idea is to take *inspired action* – we don't want to force ourselves into doing anything. When we're ready, possibilities will reveal themselves to us. We suddenly have important choices to make.

How exciting!

How scary!

Wouldn't it be nice if we could start here – the calm *after* the storm?

Be careful not to jump ahead – covering up your pain by doing things that are exciting at the moment but then end with a crash and burn.

When we try to move forward before we've said a full and genuine goodbye to the one we've lost, we only end up setting ourselves up for failure when we are reminded of them and feel guilty for moving on.

By the time you get to Phase 4, having done the deep emotional work to get here, you might not recognize yourself. You might not see how far you have come. It is difficult to track our progress through grief. I know it is a long journey.

It is also easy to give up before you complete this final phase.

I implore you not to give up! Keep going. Plant your flag in the ground and reclaim your life. Things I could not have dreamt of before were now within reach for me.

We will move out of mere survival mode here. Hard to believe, right?

So, what could your next chapter look like? For some of us, it might be time to take better care of our health. Trauma, loss, and grief can place enormous stress on our physical and mental health. Replacing some of our unhealthy coping mechanisms with healthier options will support us as we explore new opportunities.

We might dedicate ourselves to our careers. We might change careers entirely after having found a new interest or passion.

I did both. First, I leaned into my career and then decided to create something brand new that left me feeling inspired and with a newfound sense of purpose. I decided to dedicate my time to helping others through their grief. It is some of the most rewarding work of my life.

For those who have lost a life partner, I want to assure you that it is possible to experience an intimate relationship again. Our partners who have passed would want us to be happy again, to have joy and companionship in our lives.

I know Tony would want that for me.

As we heal, new opportunities will unfold for us. Yes, this might sound difficult to you right now, I know. You might be thinking, *"I don't know where to start or even what I want?"*

But with a committed willingness to work with grief, not against it, you will make it here to the Inspired Living Phase of the Life Raft Model, where you will be safely in the harbor, able to walk once again on dry land and begin to explore and experiment in a way that never would have been possible before.

Stay curious, and little by little, with every step, you will find new ideas and inspiration.

Stay the course.

Phase 4 requires courage and curiosity to walk through new doors with newfound confidence and to see life through new, wise eyes. It is about asking and exploring questions like "Where do I want to go *from here?*"

It's about accepting that you are here without wishing to be elsewhere.

Whether you like it or not, you are an entirely different person now.

Grief has changed you.

You may feel guilt or shame for even considering moving forward. But consider this: wouldn't the one you lost be so proud of you for picking up this book? That alone was an act of inspired action, without a doubt!

You're not only meant to survive – you deserve to thrive while always holding the memory of your loved one close to your heart.

Honor your grief.

Respect it.

Feel it.

It is here for you, but only as long as you are willing to heed the lessons it has to teach you.

You will stumble, so don't be surprised when it happens.

And when you succeed, celebrate!

My wish for you is that you feel fully alive again one day.

Grief does not want you to die. It wants you to live.

❧

Crossing the Ocean of Grief will be different for all of us. It will include the depths of despair and the possibility of growth in so many areas of our lives. From increased personal strength, improved relationships, new life experiences, greater appreciation for life, and spiritual growth, it is possible to experience the full range of emotions again, not just the difficult ones.

I recall once daring to look forward to peace, love, and joy.

What do you dare to look forward to?

WHERE DO WE GO FROM HERE?

On some days, grief can get pretty darn ugly. You already know this.

We experience not one loss but many.

The first loss is the death of our loved one. But then we realize the dreams we had together have died. We lose the memories that we will never make together.

We lose the places we will never visit together.

Yes, grief can get pretty ugly, but only if we never learn the beautiful value of life it is trying to show us.

※

I don't expect that you will have moved through each phase of the Life Raft Model in the short time it took you to read this book.

It is likely you remain entrenched in Phase 1.

"Where do I start?" you might be asking yourself.

You can only start where you are. Not where you think you should be or wish you could be but exactly where you are today. Right now.

What do you need? Do you even know? If you're caught up in the depths of despair, it may be impossible to know where you are.

I can help you with that. I have crossed the Ocean of Grief… and I lived to tell a story that I hope will give you hope.

But first, you'll have to do something I resisted for far too long: I needed to ask for help. The waters were just too deep, and I was so far from shore.

I needed a life raft. I suspect you may need one, too.

I wrote this book to share what I have learned because no one should have to do this alone.

Consider this book a life raft sent to you from me to guide you back to shore.

When we first set out on our grief journey, we think, feel, and behave the same way we did in our old life before our Big Loss. But everything has changed. We have changed. There's no going back to our old life, and the person we used to be doesn't fit into this new life – the one with the big gaping hole.

I needed to find new ways of being, thinking, and responding to this new so-called "life."

The old ways only served to keep me in pain.

How about you? Are you ready to ask for help?

At first, you might think, *"I can't do this. I'll never be the same."*

You're right; you'll never be the same.

I thought I would never recover. This is because I did not know how.

"How will I ever survive this?"

The best way that I have found is by following the Life Raft Model.

It is your "how."

I had no such framework to follow when I lost Tony. But the seemingly insurmountable grief I experienced after his loss — and methodically working my way through the phases that would become my Life Raft Model – inspired me to help others who find themselves drowning in despair, alone in their pain.

You are at a crossroads right now. You have a few options at this very moment.

The first option is to do nothing, succumb to grief, and wait for it to "go away."

That's right; it is your prerogative to do absolutely nothing.

You can put this book down and pretend you never read it. You may decide that working your way through the phases of the Life Raft Model seems too daunting.

I hope you don't choose this option. Waiting for grief to go away never works.

The second option would be to try to cross the Ocean of Grief alone, using what you have learned from this book. This is a much better option than the first one, but without a guide to help you steer the course, you'll likely paddle in circles and it will take a lot longer to get back on dry land, where your inspired life awaits.

Option three is to work with someone who can guide you as you cross the Ocean of Grief. This is the option I ultimately chose after attempting to do it myself.

This is the option that saved me.

If option three is your choice, I am here for you. I have crossed that ocean. And while I never thought it would be possible, I made it back onto dry land. I can show you how to do the same. If you'd like to inquire about how we might work together, visit my website at www.SandyLotzWeiner.com.

If you're truly stuck, you may find some answers by taking my **Life Raft Grief Assessment.** You'll find it on my website. It will help you assess the extent of your grief and what course of action would provide you the comfort and support you need.

I know this pain. I know it well. And so, I offer you my hand.

I am so proud of you for making it to the end of this book. You have begun the process of taking care of your needs. Your next new chapter awaits.

May it be filled with peace, love, joy, and inspiration.

WHAT GRIEF HAS TAUGHT ME

"Universe, what were you thinking?"

I was shouting at the sky as I walked the beach – something I used to love doing, but not that day.

In fact, on most days in the early stages of my grief, I longed for the past, the days before my nightmare began. At the same time, I developed a fear of the dark and the uncertain future that lay ahead of me. Eventually, I just knew that staying in my painful reality forever was not an option – at least, not for me.

"Stop! You keep walking over the bridge in your head, running between the past and the future. What if you stay in the now? Begin where you are."

And so, I began to heal, and eventually… to write.

❧

People often ask me, "Sandy, how are you?"

I know what they want to hear. I know what they want me to say. And the last thing I ever want to say to someone who is genuinely asking is, "Fine. I'm fine."

Truth is… things are more than fine now, but it took me a long time to get here.

There was a time when life without Tony wasn't even *understandable*.

Now, it's just me, and I am honestly okay. I am alive. I crossed the Ocean of Grief without knowing if I'd make it.

It's been more than six years since I lost the love of my life, and yet there are days when it feels like he's sitting right beside me. Other days, it feels like he's in the other room.

And *some* days, it's just me, and I am *thriving*. I never imagined I'd ever be able to write the word "thriving" to describe myself again.

My healing will continue, that I know. Will I ever be fully healed? I'm not even sure if that's possible. I know I am not the same woman I once was.

Grief changed me. Not for better or worse. I am simply not the same.

I have found ways to help myself reduce and resolve my pain and explore what brings me new-found pleasure. I keep looking for what inspires me now, what makes my soul come alive, and I keep doing more of what I love.

Finding sweetness in the small moments of life is a gift. I have a new appreciation for *my* life.

And I now know for sure that love never dies.

The love I had with Tony is now the glue that holds all the chapters of my life together, allowing me to feel *fully alive*.

Being of service to others is very rewarding, and I know there is more for me to experience in this world.

I have had more losses since Tony passed, *and I am still here.*

I am creating this new *next* chapter of my Inspired Life, one choice and one day at a time. Besides writing this book, I am doing work that I love, which is to coach my clients as they swim across the Ocean of Grief.

It is the most rewarding work I have ever done.

So, you see? I am alive.

Do I still miss my loved ones who have passed on? Yes, of course I do. I still love and cherish the memories I have of them.

I also know they are always with me. I ask them for guidance when I am uncertain or need reassurance. I ask for a sign, and when I progress and succeed, we celebrate together.

I know they are smiling, always cheering me on, proud of how far I have come.

২৯

Writing this book for you, dear Reader, has been yet another step on my healing journey. I felt I had a story to tell that might help others.

My story is about a woman who loved and lost and found her way through to the other side of the ocean. She found the courage to live again. It is not something that will make the evening news. But maybe, by telling my story, I can give you the hope you need.

Hope heals. Allow yourself to be inspired by everything around you.

This was my intention and my heart's desire when I wrote this book.

Writing this book took me back to some of the painful parts of my own story, and it surprised me that I could still touch the rawness of these emotions. I would do it all over again if this mighty tiny book served to give one person hope for healing.

You, too, have a story that needs to be told, no matter how you choose to tell it.

I hope you will share it with me one day.

I am here should you ever need me.

ACKNOWLEDGMENTS

I would like to thank my Loved Ones who have passed away:

My beloved husband Tony, Mom and Dad, Nikita and Ms. Cleo, our fur babies. Thank you for the love you gave me and for continuing to guide me from afar. I will always love you. I promise to keep looking for the sweet moments in life and do more of what inspires me and makes my heart smile.

Thank you to all my Earth Angels:

The Team at MTBA, Lin, Dustin, Rhianon, Caroline & the rest of the team. Thank you for supporting me to make this a reality, I could not have done this without you.

To all who have been my support and pillars of strength during the passing of Tony:

My family: Arno, Alta, Louise, Pieter, Dani, Ilse, Maya, Dylan, Jethro, Chris, Caron, Daniel, Lexi, Lauren, Scarlet, Ella, Phil, Kerry, Merle, Michael, and Ceren, you kept me going when I did not want to.

My Monterey Village Family: Dean, Keith, Kala, Therese, Rosanne, Nicole, Shawn and Khanh, Stephanie and David, Ian and Addison, and Charlotte, for being great neighbors and for your kind support.

My USA family of friends: Nancy and Jim, Cathy, Renee M, Cindy, Claudia and Phil, Michele and Alan, Suzy, Melina, Valerie, Janine and Roger, Renee N, Rhonda, Lani, Robert, Julie, Hilda, Diane, Carmelita, Monica, for walking beside me throughout my grief.

Monterey Bay Rosen Method Center, Jane and Melina for taking care of me that day.

My Lucky family and co-workers in Carmel and Sand City, you were there every day; thank you.

Midnite Express, Tony's band: Michael T, Alan and Mike K for the tribute video.

The South African Expat community of Monterey Peninsula for showing up.

SAWITU (South African Women in The USA and Canada) for your inspiration.

Rabbi David and Congregation Beth Israel for helping me give Tony the burial he wanted.

My South African friends and family, Colleen, Diane, Vera, Marina, Christa, Wilma, Theresa, Elmien, and many more, you always make me feel welcome and loved.

My Grief Support Team: Helen Grady MFT, Annemarie at Grief

and Trauma Healing Network, David Kessler Grief Educator Program, Julie Cluff, Build a Life after Loss Coaching for giving me the pieces I needed to Grieve Fully.

Michael Jeter, my personal Trainer, for helping me find my strength and my confidence.

Arthur Murray Monterey Teachers and Students, for helping me find my rhythm.

Greg and the Dedman family for opening your hearts and your homes to me during COVID.

LeTip Carmel, for supporting me in building my Grief Coaching business, I appreciate all of you.

To my pharmacy and coaching clients for teaching me every day about resilience.

For the kindness of strangers, you have been life savers.

And to you, dear Reader, for buying and reading this book.

I am deeply grateful to each and every one of you for helping me through my darkest hours and for supporting others by supporting me in doing this work.

Love and Light to you all.

In deep gratitude,
Sandy

ABOUT THE AUTHOR

Sandy Lotz-Weiner is a Grief Coach and Educator.

She is also a bereaved wife, daughter, and immigrant.

Sandy started her professional career as a pharmacist in South Africa, her country of birth. In 2003, she relocated with her late husband, Tony, to the beautiful Monterey Peninsula in California. There, she worked as a pharmacist and obtained her credentials as a Health and Life Coach, working with clients part-time.

In 2017, with the passing of her husband and then her mother, Sandy became interested in studying grief and the grieving process. After she moved through her grief journey, she became a certified Grief Coach and Educator.

As she would say: *"First, I did the practical, and then I studied the theory."*

Sandy still lives on the Monterey Peninsula today.

To contact Sandy or to take her *Life Raft Grief Assessment,* please visit

www.SandyLotzWeiner.com

Published by AFGO Press
AFGOpress.com

Made in the USA
Middletown, DE
07 November 2023

42134424R00056